F R A N K
L L O Y D
W R I G H T
S T A I N E D
G L A S S
P O R T F O L I O

Text & Photographs by
Thomas A. Heinz

GIBBS·SMITH
P
PUBLISHER

SALT LAKE CITY

I owe a great debt to architect Al Drap for first introducing me to the work of Mr. Wright and, in particular, the stained glass. His interest, knowledge, and enthusiasm has had a deep and lasting effect on me. It is greatly appreciated. Thank you, Al.

The work in this book was supported in part by a fellowship from the National Endowment for the Arts.

96 95 94 93 8 7 6 5 4 3 2 1
Text and photographs copyright © 1993 by Thomas A. Heinz

This is a Peregrine Smith Book, published by
Gibbs Smith, Publisher
P.O. Box 667
Layton, Utah 84041

Cover photograph: Susan Lawrence Dana House, Ballroom Ceiling Light,
    ©1993 by Thomas A. Heinz
Design by J. Scott Knudsen, Park City, Utah
Printed by Regent Publishing Services, Hong Kong

Library of Congress Cataloging-in-Publication Data
Heinz, Thomas A.
Frank Lloyd Wright portfolio. Stained glass / Thomas A. Heinz.
p. cm.
ISBN 0-87905-590-1
1. Wright, Frank Lloyd, 1867–1959—Themes, motives. 2. Glass painting and staining—United States—Themes, motives. I. Title.
NK5398.W78H45 1993
748.5913—dc20   93-14075
                         CIP

FRANK LLOYD WRIGHT'S DESIGNS for stained, or art, glass were geometric abstractions of things that are familiar, such as the tulip of the Bradley windows and the many wildflowers of the Dana House. His creations were designed "in the nature of the materials," specifically glass and metal. With an understanding that each piece of glass would be surrounded by came (the name of the metal used to hold the glass together), Wright saw both the graphic and structural applications. He knew that L- and T-shaped glass would break across the inside corners, so with his T square and triangle he created regular polygons. And looking for ways to control production costs, he used straight lines rather than curves, because straight lines were easier to cut.

The materials used by Wright were as inventive and new as the designs themselves. Although lead had been the metal commonly used for came, Wright found that precise, straight lines could be achieved by using stiffer metals such as zinc, copper and brass.

Wright dealt with windows and their designs as "light screens." He found that glass with a coating of metal on it produced an iridescence; the intensity of the colors changed with the differing light conditions. The color of glass is dependent on different chemicals. Green comes from copper and blue from cobalt. Glass chemists also use silver and uranium. Wright sought out these combinations that produced uncommon colors.

His earliest patterns were quite traditional, such as those used in the dining room of his own Oak Park House in the late 1890s. The bay windows of the Bradley House just a few years later took a dramatic step into the geometric abstraction of plants.

The most unusual experiment during these early years was in the east end of the ballroom of the Dana House. The semicircular plate glass acts as a weather shield, keeping out the wind and rain. Inside, hung from a wood frame, are many individual, unframed sections of art glass. By the time of the Mrs. Thomas Gale House of 1909 in Oak Park, the patterns were quite minimalist. Designing both in abstraction and minimalist continued until his last house with stained-glass windows—the Ennis House of 1924 in Los Angeles.

Experimentation in glass extended into mosaics (Husser House, D. D. Martin House and Ennis House) and Pyrex tubing (Johnson Wax Building). The final experiment in light screens came with the introduction of cut-wood screens such as those used in most of the Usonian houses starting in the late 1930s. They were much less costly and could be executed on the job site by the finish carpenter. These screens cast ever-changing shadow patterns that drifted throughout the rooms as the sun rose and set each day.

Seeing the evolving effects of Wright's glass artworks firsthand allows an appreciation for his genius. The patterns, materials, and applications take them far beyond our expectations, and yet the colors and scale make them familiar to us in many ways.

Thomas A. Heinz
Evanston, Illinois
June 1992

B. Harley Bradley House,
Dining Room Ceiling Lights

I t is unfortunate that these ceiling lights have been removed and sold at auction. They are about the earliest of the Prairie-era designs. The winged motif likely comes from Wright's and Orlando Giannini's interests in the American Indian motifs. The mural in the playroom in Wright's Oak Park House has a similar design. This design seems busy and not very refined—too many lines. It is noteworthy that when the panels are inverted, there is a continuity to the pattern.

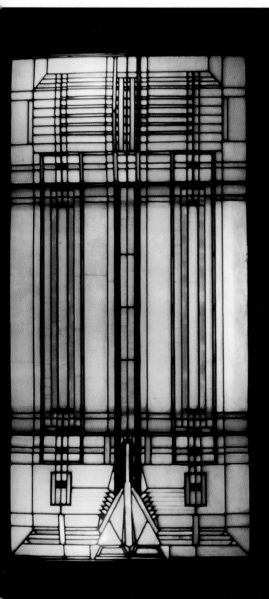

B. Harley Bradley House, Living Room Bay Window

The diagonal lines of the pattern are at the same pitch as the lines of the roof. In that regard, the windows relate directly to their setting and would appear to fit in only one building—this one. The relationship between panes, in this case, is vertical, not side-to-side. There are very small red glass highlights strategically placed to make the windows sparkle.

WARREN HICKOX HOUSE, FRONT BAY WINDOWS

As with its next-door neighbor—the B. Harley Bradley House—the diagonals of the glass pattern duplicate the roof pitch. While the orientation of the individual patterns and the white glass bars is vertical, the overall effect of the set is horizontal.

FRANK THOMAS HOUSE, ENTRY CEILING LIGHTS

Wright's sense of experimentation with patterns and materials is visible here. The long triangles are carryovers from the patterns for the windows of the house. In the four corners of this pattern is a most unusual material. The texture in quadrants is mother-of-pearl glued to glass. As far as is known, this is the only example of layering used in any of Wright's glass work. It is a miracle that none of these pieces of shell has ever come loose.

FRANK THOMAS HOUSE, ENTRY VESTIBULE

A double reverse entry sequence is a most delightful experience. The entry doors are unexpectedly at diagonally opposite sides of the vestibule. Surrounded by sparkling gold mirror glass in seven full-height stained-glass doors, one is nearly disoriented by the spectacle.

WARD WILLITS HOUSE, LIVING ROOM WINDOW

Copper came is used in these simple and innovative windows. The copper has been blackened. It is not clear if the came was treated or if it is a gradual natural process. Since the Willits lived in the house for over fifty years, it was maintained very well. There are only three kinds of glass used in the windows: clear plate, white milk, and gold mirror glass.

WILLIAM E. MARTIN HOUSE, ENTRY CEILING LIGHT

U sing only squares and rectangles, Wright's mastery of simple patterns is beautifully expressed in this example. The nature of the materials is also brought to its limits. The joinery of the metal cames at the corners of the central squares takes a special understanding of exactly how the glass would have to be cut to fit well.

Susan Lawrence Dana House, Master Bedroom Sumac

E very wall of the Dana House is embellished with a different art-glass pattern. The theme running throughout is a stemmed flower. In this example, it is expressed as a series of herringbone chevrons; some are rectangular and some are triangular. The bold triangular ones that dominate this set appear to have a third dimension. Each piece of glass is a simple geometric shape: a square, rectangle, diamond, or triangle.

19

SUSAN LAWRENCE DANA HOUSE, FRONT DOOR FAN LIGHT, DETAIL

T he butterfly is the only example in an art-glass window of Wright using anything other than a plant form. The glass used in this light is very special. From the outside, with reflected light, it has hues of blue and green. An application of metal salts was fired onto the glass, causing the iridescence. From the inside, with transmitted light, the color of the glass is a straw amber. These two combinations change as the light changes, making each day a new experience.

SUSAN LAWRENCE DANA HOUSE, FRONT ENTRY FAN LIGHT AND BARREL VAULT

Compared with the photograph on page 21, you can see the difference of the transmitted light vs. the reflected light. There is a second fan light just above where the camera is taking this photograph. The barrel vault connects the two.

Susan Lawrence Dana House, North Library Window

The flower-with-stem pattern is consistent with those of the rest of the house, but the use of variable came widths has been eliminated here. The green and orange glass are colors of the prairie plants that Wright used in virtually all of his art-glass work.

Susan Lawrence Dana House, Dining Room Sumac Window, Detail

T he variations found in nature that keep it from becoming boring are found here in Wright's design. Wright establishes a pattern and rhythm and then breaks it. The Dana House budget was quite large and allowed for expensive stained-glass patterns such as this. Another compelling aspect of these windows is Wright's ability to observe and understand the proportion and pattern of each plant, such that he was able to abstract the essential elements and bring them into the windows as something new and yet familiar.

SUSAN LAWRENCE DANA HOUSE, FOUNTAIN SIDE LIGHT

As with the photograph on page 23, the flower-with-stem is the basis for this pattern. Here, though, the heavy camed squares are a carryover of the trellislike frames of the fountain doors. Even taken out of context, it is still a strong and effective design.

SUSAN LAWRENCE DANA HOUSE, BALLROOM CEILING LIGHT

T he angles of the fireplace facing are repeated in the dynamic diagonals of this ceiling light. The crossed sets of cames creates a positive tension that makes it an exciting design. The overall yellow cast of the glass creates a warm glow on the fireplace below, even when there is no fire.

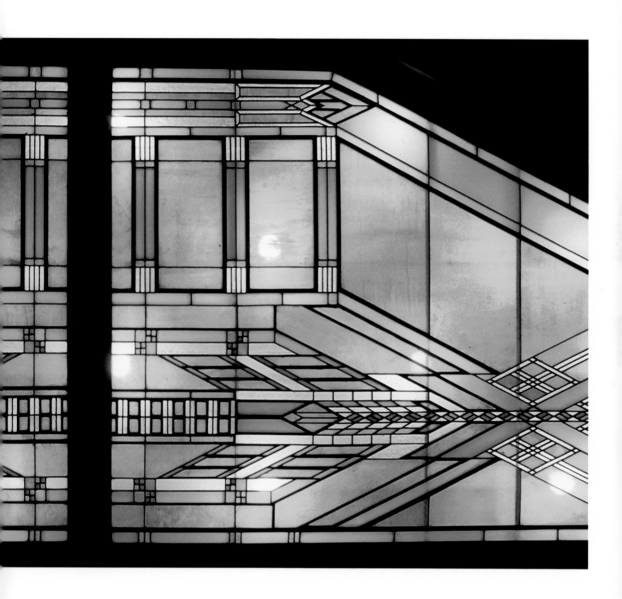

SUSAN LAWRENCE DANA HOUSE, FERNERY HALL DOORS

The delicate nature of ferns is expressed in this pattern without literally reproducing the color or the exact pattern of the fronds. The pattern does seem to hang from the top of the door and trail down to the bottom. When the eye focuses on the glass pattern, the objects beyond become obscured. This seems to be the trick that works on Wright's light screens and keeps indoors private without resorting to drapes.

SUSAN LAWRENCE DANA HOUSE, FOUNTAIN DOORS AND WINDOWS

These doors and windows comprise the finest set of art glass in Wright's career. This is the most brilliant example of his understanding of the balance between repetition and consistency found in nature. The two sets of doors at either side of the fountain are similar but not symmetrical. Each carries the rhythm of the other without being mirror images. When seen in person, the white band at the top of the series of doors and windows gets a bit lost.

FRANCIS LITTLE HOUSE, FRONT ENTRY DOOR

A near duplicate of the fan light of the Dana House, this unit contains only gold mirror and clear glass. The brass came has acquired a black patina from the air pollution. The cast stone surrounding the fan light overwhelms it in proportion and projection. The door glass pattern is not completely successful in tying the fan light pattern to it. The drawings for both this house and the Dana House from nearby Springfield are originated and revised on exactly the same dates. Little wonder the designs are parallel.

J. J. WALSER HOUSE, LIVING ROOM WINDOW

This motif was a favorite of Frank Lloyd Wright. It was begun in the Dana House windows (pages 25, 29), and variations appear in the Barton House (page 41).

GEORGE BARTON HOUSE, EAST FRONT LIVING ROOM WINDOWS

A design based on the typical "Chicago window," consisting of a large center light and side ventilating units, is used in this residential setting. The pattern in the sidelights is quite similar to the window from the Dana House (page 25) as are the upper and lower wall sconces. These sconces were designed by Walter Burley Griffin and were used in several Wright-designed houses.

ARTHUR HEURTLEY HOUSE, LIVING ROOM CEILING LIGHT

A skylight has glass that is illuminated by daylight from the top and illuminated at night by light bulbs from behind in its own light box. The lights are turned off in this photograph to show the different glass colors. The profile of the house is repeated upside down twice in each of the two ceiling lights.

WILLIAM R. HEATH HOUSE, STAIRWAY WINDOW, SECOND FLOOR

Many of Wright's art-glass windows use the same types and colors of glass. The wide glass bands that come in from both sides continue in adjacent windows, some as long as five units. Mr. Heath was the attorney for the Larkin Company.

FREDERICK ROBIE HOUSE, SOUTH LIVING ROOM DOORS

The wood grilles in the ceiling are wooden light screens, as are the art-glass doors in the wall. The soft light cast by the bulbs above the grilles became known as moonlight to the residents. The patterns of the windows are curious because of the lack of detail at the bottom. This may have been a result of them being designed to be seen from the front walk, with the bottom being obscured by the low parapet wall at the balcony. This argument is strengthened by the pattern in the window to the right.

OSCAR STEFFENS HOUSE, LIVING ROOM WINDOW

Very few of Wright's stained-glass windows have blue glass. The Steffens is an exception. It is very likely that the blue was a request of the client, since it is the client that pays for the house.

AVERY COONLEY HOUSE, WOOD CEILING GRILLE

This unit is the center panel of a band of these ceiling lights that extends around three sides of the living room just above the window line. The pattern here is made from wood and replaces the glass and metal of the art-glass panels that would otherwise be in these locations. The three-dimensional effects of the overlapping pieces could not have been easily constructed in glass and came.

HARRY ADAMS HOUSE, SOUTH FRONT DOOR

The random squares of iridescent glass in the front door are enlivened by the observer's movement past the door. Because the little squares are set at slightly different angles, they reflect light at different positions, making a dynamic display. At this point in his work, Wright's decorative work became more random, not as tight and orderly as it had been.

F. C. Bogk House, Sun Room Windows

The attention to detail in all aspects of design is shown in the restrained example. The alternating squares of gold and white glass, with the occasional came tie uniting the two borders, is simple and reminiscent of Japanese design.

John Storer House, Concrete Block

Wright's light screens have gone through many variations. They started as art glass and later evolved into wood screens. In the Storer House and in other concrete-block houses in the Los Angeles area, the light screens became decorative concrete blocks. Some of these blocks had light bulbs illuminating them and others, in groups, were glazed as windows.

CHARLES ENNIS HOUSE, GLASS MOSAIC OVERMANTLE

Not all of Frank Lloyd Wright's glass work was bound by metal came. The two glass mosaics of his Prairie years were both executed by Orlando Giannini and were quite similar in design to the Ennis House pattern. Since they both lived in La Jolla at the time of the construction of this house, it is conceivable that Wright located Giannini and employed him on this project.

CHARLES ENNIS HOUSE, LIVING ROOM WINDOW

*T*he Ennis House is the last of Wright's houses to have art-glass windows. These patterns are again abstractions of plants—desert plants that were prevalent in Los Angeles at the time. The cathedral, or colored glass, has very subtle color variations. From the top to the bottom of the central motif, the colors become lighter.

S. C. Johnson Wax Administration Building, Pyrex Window

W right had an amazing ability to make art out of mundane materials. At the Johnson Wax Building, he curved the glass tubes to add a third dimension. Even the joints between the individual tubes is handled artistically. Wright rarely left anything to chance or to the contractor. He conceived of the structure in its entirety and at every level of detail.

❦ These properties are open for public tours.